GW01374981

SEE HOW IT WORKS

CARS

Tony Potter

Illustrated by
Robin Lawrie

Cover design
Patrick Knowles

For Ben and Jamie

Collins

Contents

3 Linda's car
5 Under the bonnet
7 Inside the car
8 Lots of cars
10 Kinds of cars
12 At the garage
14 Car wash
16 Loading up
18 Towing
20 Breakdown
22 Car words
24 Index

Potter, Tony
Cars
1. Cars. Operation
I. Title II. Lawrie, Robin III. Series
629.28'3

ISBN 0-00-190048-X

William Collins Sons & Co Ltd
London · Glasgow · Sydney · Auckland
Toronto · Johannesburg

First Published in Great Britain 1989
© William Collins Sons & Co Ltd 1989

All rights reserved. No part of this publication may be reproduced, stored in a retrieval system, or transmitted, in any form or by any means, electronic, mechanical, photocopying, recording or otherwise, without the prior permission of William Collins Sons & Co Ltd, 8 Grafton Street, LONDON W1X 3LA

Printed and bound in Singapore

Inside the car

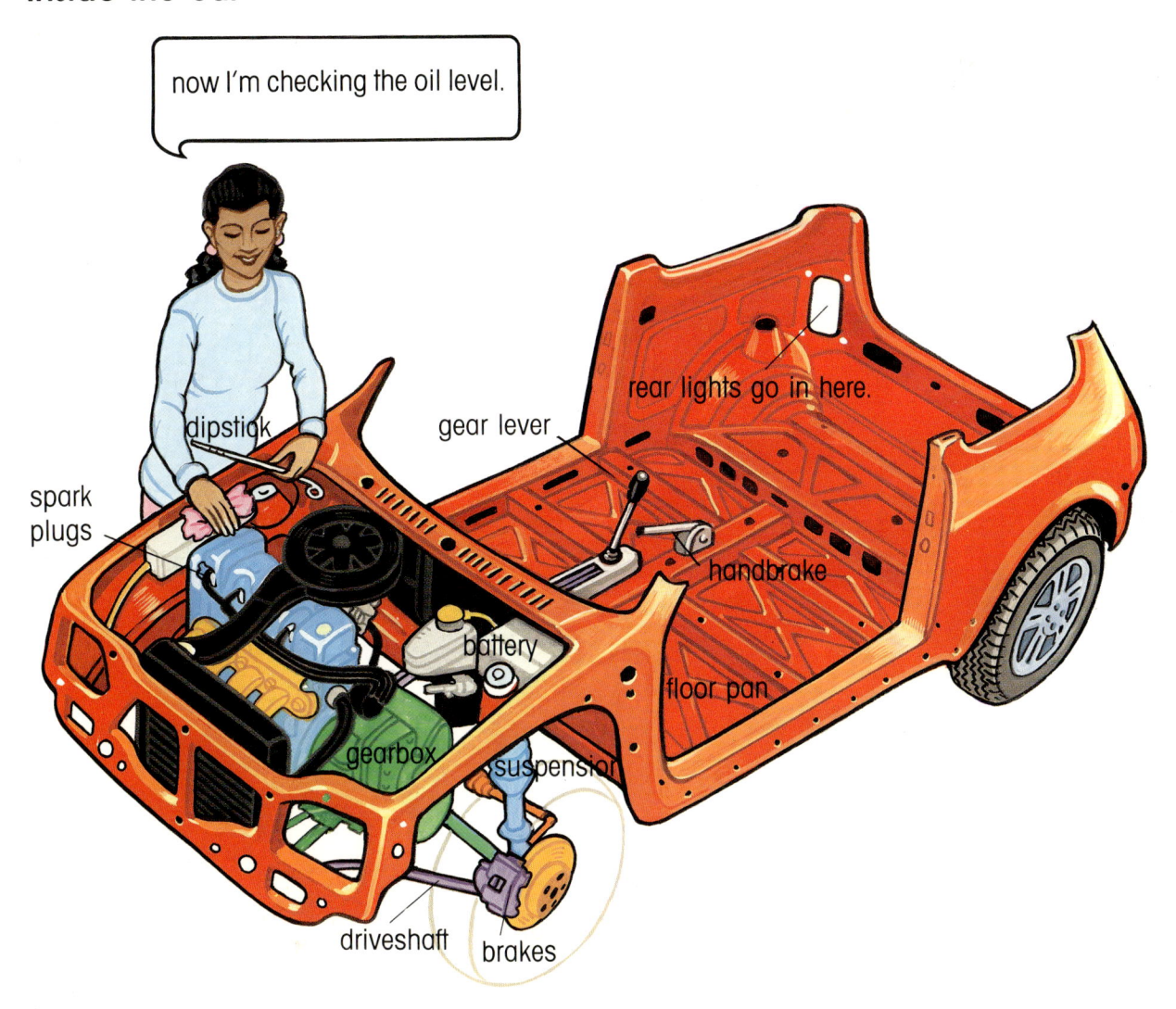

now I'm checking the oil level.

dipstick

spark plugs

gear lever

rear lights go in here.

handbrake

battery

floor pan

gearbox

suspension

driveshaft   brakes

The part you can see now is called the chassis.

Lots of cars

Citroen 2CV
Lotus
BMW
Lincoln
Toyota 4 WD
police car
Fiat X 19
Lamborghini Countach
rally car
Cadillac

Here is a giant traffic jam! See how many of these cars you can spot outdoors.

8

Porsche
E-Type Jaguar
racing car
stretched limousine
Porsche
MG TC
hot rod
Rolls Royce
Metro
Land Rover
Volkswagen Beetle

Kinds of cars

George likes to drive his veteran car for fun.

Chris drives a small hatchback to get to work.

Hari has a family saloon.

This picture shows the main kinds of cars you can get. People need cars for different reasons. Some people just like to have fun. Other people need a car for work. Which kind of car would you like to have?

Anne needs an estate car to carry heavy loads.

Di likes to go fast in her sports car.

Ben needs a four-wheel drive car for his farm.

11

At the garage

petrol pump

air line

Tom is checking the oil.

The Jackson family are at the garage. Pete is checking the tyres to make sure they have enough air in them. Janet is filling the tank up with petrol.

welding equipment

screwdriver

open-ended spanner

ramps   mallet

pneumatic spanner

Jamie is a mechanic. He is underneath the car fixing the steering.

He is standing in a special hole in the ground which gives him room to work.

Car wash

brushes

soapy water

Some people like to clean their car in a car wash. Soapy water is sprayed all over the body. Then huge brushes scrub the car clean.

Mike likes to wash his car at home. First he cleans it with a soapy sponge. Then he rinses all the soap off with a hosepipe.

Loading up

bikes

roof rack

case

paddle

rucksacks

canoe

Robin is loading the back of his estate car ready to go on holiday.

He puts long things and big things on the roof rack.

16

Farmer Bill's sheepdog is herding sheep into his four-wheel drive car.

There is a special ramp for the sheep to go up.

ramp

Towing

horse box

Helen tows a horse box with her car. The horse box fixes on a hook at the back called a tow bar. She has to drive very carefully.

18

scramble bike

Phil pulls a trailer with his four-wheel drive Jeep. You can load all kinds of things in trailers. Phil has a scramble bike in his trailer.

Breakdown

hatchback

wing

nuts

jack

spanner

wheel trim

spare tyre

Sometimes things go wrong with cars. Harry's hatchback has a puncture.

He has a spare tyre to use instead of the one with the puncture.

breakdown truck

skid marks

This car has crashed into a tree and smashed the front wing.

A breakdown truck has come to tow it away to the garage.

Car words

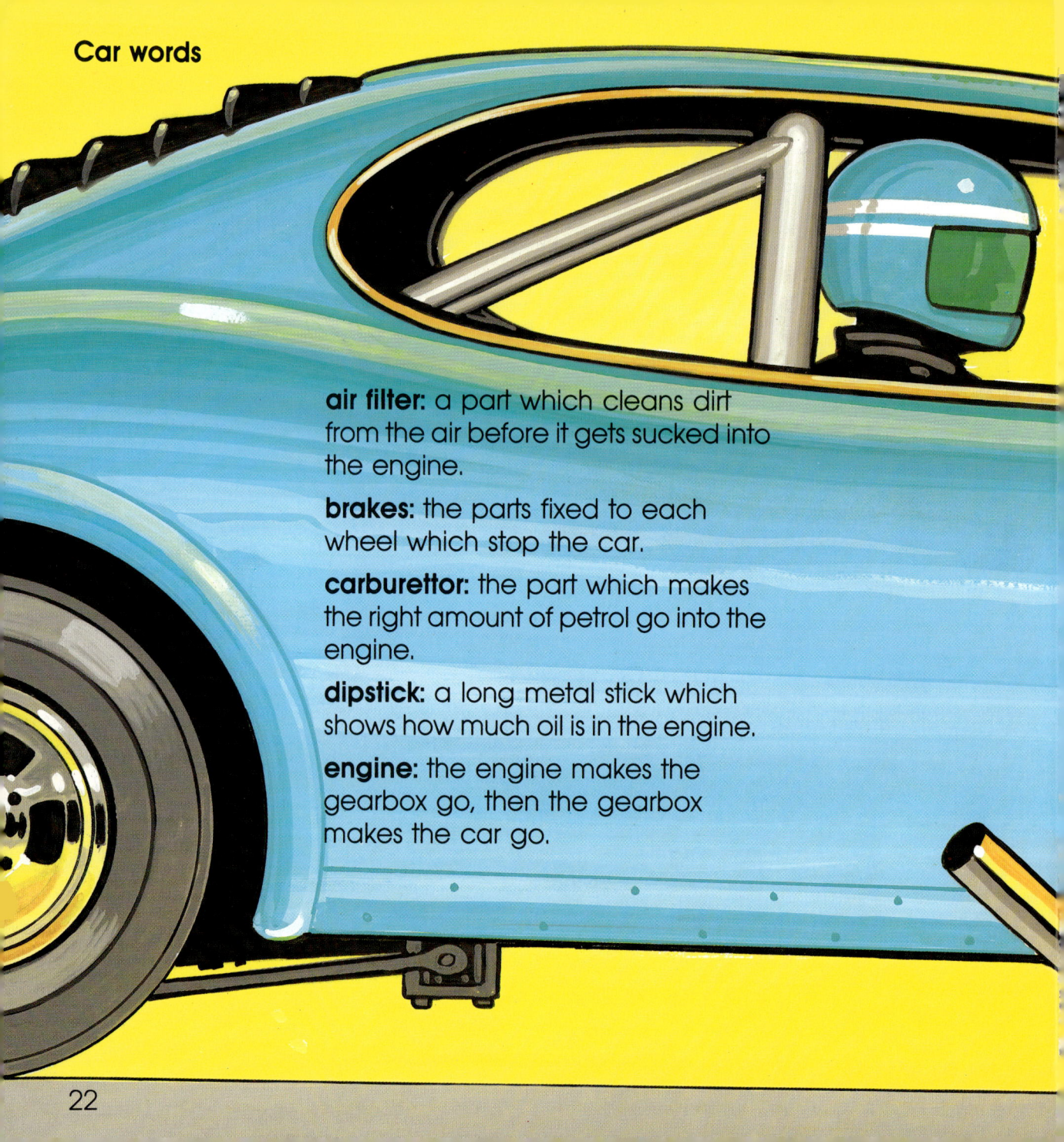

air filter: a part which cleans dirt from the air before it gets sucked into the engine.

brakes: the parts fixed to each wheel which stop the car.

carburettor: the part which makes the right amount of petrol go into the engine.

dipstick: a long metal stick which shows how much oil is in the engine.

engine: the engine makes the gearbox go, then the gearbox makes the car go.

gearbox: the part of a car which makes the engine's power turn the front or back wheels.

nearside: the side of the car nearest the kerb.

offside: the driver's side of the car.

radiator: the part of a car which cools the water flowing round the engine.

suspension: the parts fixed to each wheel which make a car springy.